Forgive the Past – L
Live the Present – the P
Create the Future – Thought

Great Brita
Get Up And Go Diary 2013

Messages
of hope and encouragement

Wisdom
from yesterday for today and tomorrow

Humour
to make you smile when you are down

Optimism
for you to see the brighter side of life

Thoughts
of gratitude for what you value and appreciate

Inspiration
for when you want it

Motivation
for when you need it

Space
for you to invent your own goals and dreams

For Tommy – My Inspiration

Missing someone isn't about how long its
been since you've seen them last or the
amount of time since you've talked.
Its about that very moment when you're
doing something and you wish that they
were right there with you.

Glenda

Published in 2012 by Get Up And Go Publications Ltd.

ISBN 978-0-9554223-7-9

Design and Origination: Glenda Devlin

Cover Photo: Catriona Shatwell
www.doublevision-images.com

Graphic Design by Printfix, Sligo
Printed in UK

Published by
GET UP AND GO PUBLICATIONS LTD
8 Burma Road, Strandhill,
Co. Sligo, Ireland

Website: www.getupandgodiary.com
Email: info@getupandgodiary.com

Sligo
Land of Heart's Desire

"I love quotations because it is a joy
to find thoughts one might have,
beautifully expressed with much authority,
by someone recognised as wiser than oneself".
Marlene Dietrich

"Everyday you may make progress.
Every step may be fruitful.
Yet there will stretch out before you an
ever lengthening, ever acsending, ever improving path.
You know you will never get to the end of the journey.
But this, so far from discouraging,
only adds to the joy and the glory of the climb".

Winston Chruchill

This Diary Belongs To: _____

Address: _____

Telephone: _____

Email: _____

"Books say: "She did this because".
Life says: "She did this".
Books are where things are explained to you.
Life is where things aren't.
I'm not surprised some people prefer books".
Julian Barnes

EMERGENCY TELEPHONE NUMBERS

_____

_____

_____

Your diary contains 140 pages of inspiration! **Enjoy every page!**

BANK AND PUBLIC HOLIDAYS 2013

ENGLAND, SCOTLAND, WALES

New Years Day 1 January; 2 January (Scotland) **Good Friday** 29 March;
Easter Monday 1 April; **May Holiday** 6 May; **Spring Bank Holiday** 27 May.
Summer Bank Holiday 26 August; **Christmas Day** 25 December;
Boxing Day 26 December.

NORTHERN IRELAND

New Years Day 1 January; **St Patrick's Day** 1 7 (18) March;
Good Friday 29 March; **Easter Monday** 1 April; **May Holiday** 6 May;
Spring Bank Holiday 27 May; **Orangeman's Day** 12 July;
Summer Bank Holiday 26 August; **Christmas Day** 25 December;
Boxing Day 26 December.

REPUBLIC OF IRELAND

New Years Day 1 January; **St Patrick's Day** 17 (18) March;
Good Friday 29 March; **Easter Monday** 1 April; **May Holiday** 6 May;
June Holiday 3 June; **August Holiday** 5 August;
October Holiday 28 October; **Christmas Day** 25 December;
St Stephen's Day 26 December.

UNITED STATES OF AMERICA

New Years Day 1 January; **Martin Luther King Day** 15 January;
Presidents Day 18 February; **Memorial Day** 27 May;
Independence Day 4 July; **Labour Day** 2 September;
Columbus Day 14 October; **Veterans Day** 1 1 November;
Thanksgiving 28 November; **Christmas Day** 25 December.

CANADA

New Years Day 1 January; **Heritage Day** 18 February;
Family Day 18 February; **Commonwealth Day** 11 March,
St Patricks Day 17 March; **Good Friday** 29 March;
Easter Monday 1 April; **Victoria Day** 25 May; **Canada Day** 1 July;
Labour Day 2 September; **Thanksgiving Day** 14 October;
Rememberance Day 1 1 November **Christmas Day** 25 December;
Boxing Day 26 December.

2013

Jan 2013

S	M	T	W	T	F	S
		1	2	3	4	5
6	7	8	9	10	11	12
13	14	15	16	17	18	19
20	21	22	23	24	25	26
27	28	29	30	31		

Feb 2013

S	M	T	W	T	F	S
					1	2
3	4	5	6	7	8	9
10	11	12	13	14	15	16
17	18	19	20	21	22	23
24	25	26	27	28		

Mar 2013

S	M	T	W	T	F	S
					1	2
3	4	5	6	7	8	9
10	11	12	13	14	15	16
17	18	19	20	21	22	23
24	25	26	27	28	29	30
31						

Apr 2013

S	M	T	W	T	F	S
	1	2	3	4	5	6
7	8	9	10	11	12	13
14	15	16	17	18	19	20
21	22	23	24	25	26	27
28	29	30				

May 2013

S	M	T	W	T	F	S
			1	2	3	4
5	6	7	8	9	10	11
12	13	14	15	16	17	18
19	20	21	22	23	24	25
26	27	28	29	30	31	

Jun 2013

S	M	T	W	T	F	S
						1
2	3	4	5	6	7	8
9	10	11	12	13	14	15
16	17	18	19	20	21	22
23	24	25	26	27	28	29
30						

Jul 2013

S	M	T	W	T	F	S
	1	2	3	4	5	6
7	8	9	10	11	12	13
14	15	16	17	18	19	20
21	22	23	24	25	26	27
28	29	30	31			

Aug 2013

S	M	T	W	T	F	S
				1	2	3
4	5	6	7	8	9	10
11	12	13	14	15	16	17
18	19	20	21	22	23	24
25	26	27	28	29	30	31

Sep 2013

S	M	T	W	T	F	S
1	2	3	4	5	6	7
8	9	10	11	12	13	14
15	16	17	18	19	20	21
22	23	24	25	26	27	28
29	30					

Oct 2013

S	M	T	W	T	F	S
		1	2	3	4	5
6	7	8	9	10	11	12
13	14	15	16	17	18	19
20	21	22	23	24	25	26
27	28	29	30	31		

Nov 2013

S	M	T	W	T	F	S
					1	2
3	4	5	6	7	8	9
10	11	12	13	14	15	16
17	18	19	20	21	22	23
24	25	26	27	28	29	30

Dec 2013

S	M	T	W	T	F	S
1	2	3	4	5	6	7
8	9	10	11	12	13	14
15	16	17	18	19	20	21
22	23	24	25	26	27	28
29	30	31				

Goals for January

 Duty makes us do things well, and love makes us do them beautifully.

January

This is a New Year

We will open the book.
Its pages are blank.
We are going to put words on them ourselves.
The book is called Opportunity
And its first chapter starts on New Year's Day.
Fill up the pages with possitivity and achievement.

**This bright new year is given me,
To live each day with zest
To daily grow and try to be
My highest and my best.**

William Arthur Ward

TUESDAY 1

New Years Day is Everyman's Birthday

WEDNESDAY 2

Remain curious about life

January

Use your imagination, not to scare yourself to death, but to inspire yourself to live.

Brookman

THURSDAY 3

Love yourself just the way you are

FRIDAY 4

Go somewhere new

SATURDAY 5

It's okay to make mistakes

SUNDAY 6

There is sanctuary in being alone with nature

Today

...like a Sunrise ... of Hope, of Prosperity, of Happiness

...'s like a New Beginning ... of Thoughts, of Words, of Actions

...'s like a New Day ... of Energy, of Strength, of Ideas

...'s like a Whole Bunch of new things ... of Prayers, of Friends, of Love.

January

MONDAY 7

Visualize a great future

TUESDAY 8

Let go of anger, resentment, and regret

WEDNESDAY 9

Keep active

Life is too short to wake up with regrets.
So love the people who treat you right,
forget about the ones who don't.
Believe everything happens for a reason.
If you get a second chance, grab it with
both hands. If it changes your life, let it.
Nobody said life would be easy,
they just said it would be worth it,

You will see it
when you believe it.

We make a living by what we get, We make a life by what we give
Winston Churchill

Pleasure in the job puts perfection in the work
Aristotle

I am thankful for ...

Throughout my life

I've loved

I've feared

I've hurt

I've lost

I've missed

I've trusted

I've made mistakes

I've laughed

I've cried

I've worried

I've lied

But most of all

I've lived

not died.

The Wolf Credo

Respect the elders

Teach the young

Cooperate with the pack

Play when you can

Hunt when you must

Rest in between

Share your affections

Voice your feelings

Leave your mark

Del Goetz

Learn to appreciate what you have,
before time makes you appreciate what you had

To handle yourself,
use your head.
To handle others,
use your heart.

The empires of the future are the empires of the mind

January

We would never learn
to be brave or patient
if there were only
joy in the world.
Helen Keller

THURSDAY 10

You do not need the approval of others

FRIDAY 11

Value yourself

SATURDAY 12

Forgiving another is your gift to yourself

SUNDAY 13

Take a risk

*It is only when we truly know, and understand,
that we have a limited time on earth,
and that we have no way of knowing when our time is up
that we will begin to live each day to the fullest,
as if it were the only one we had.*
Elizabeth Kubler-Ross

January

Courage is the force that creates history.

Life is a balance of holding on and letting go

MONDAY 14

Have a conversation that makes a difference

TUESDAY 15

Think positive thoughts

WEDNESDAY 16

Choose good habits

Appreciate again and again, freshly and naively,
the basic goods of life, with awe,
pleasure, wonder and even ecstasy,
however stale these experiences
may have become to others.

Abraham Maslow

**When you change the way you look at things,
the things you look at change.**

 January

**We are
Divine enough to ask,
and we are
Important enough
to receive.**
Wayne Dyer

THURSDAY 17

Share the goodness of life with everyone you meet

FRIDAY 18

Forgive someone for something

SATURDAY 19

Challenge your firmly held beliefs

SUNDAY 20

Accept others as they are

**The difference between school and life?
In school, you're taught a lesson
and then given a test.
In life, you're given a test
that teaches you a lesson.**
Tom Bodett

January

MONDAY 21

Kindness starts with SELF

I have been in many places, but I have never been in Cahoots.
Apparently you can't go there alone.
You have to be in Cahoots with someone.
I've also never been in Cognito.
I hear no one recognises you there.
However, I have been in Sane.
They don't have an airport, you have to be driven there.
I have made several trips thanks to my family and my work.
I would love to get to Conclusions but you have to jump,
and I'm not much into physical activity!!

TUESDAY 22

In everything you do, there is an opportunity to excel

The thoughts you have thought,
and the decisions and choices
you have made, have brought you
to where you are now.

The price of greatness is responsibility

January

The best way to find yourself is to lose yourself in the service of others.

Mahatma Gandhi

WEDNESDAY 23

Write down your ideas

THURSDAY 24

Dance with life... enjoy each step along the way

FRIDAY 25
Burns Night

Every day is a day to have a positive attitude

SATURDAY 26

Simplify your needs, simplify your life

SUNDAY 27

Have faith in your fellow man

The worst sin toward our fellow creatures is not to hate them, but to be indifferent to them; that is the essence of inhumanity.

George Bernard Shaw

Life

Life is an opportunity - benefit from it
Life is beauty - admire it
Life is bliss - taste it
Life is a dream - realise it
Life is a challenge - meet it
Life is a duty – complete it
Life is a game – play it
Life is costly - care for it
Life is wealth - value it
Life is a mystery - know it
Life is a promise - fulfil it
Life is a sorrow - overcome it
Life is a song - sing it
Life is a struggle - accept it
Life is a tragedy - confront it
Life is an adventure - dare it
Life is luck - make it
Life is precious - do not destroy it
Life is life - fight for it!

Mother Teresa

It's how you deal with failure that determines how you deal with success.
David Feberty

If you don't live for something, you will die for nothing.

January

Trustworthiness

Anyone who doesn't take truth seriously in small matters, cannot be trusted in large matters either.

Albert Einstein

MONDAY 28

Practice makes perfect

TUESDAY 29

Never give up on your dreams

WEDNESDAY 30

All is well in the world

THURSDAY 31

Celebrate the miracles of life

If you begin to understand what you are without trying to change it, then what you are, undergoes a transformation.

R Krisnamutrhy

Success is getting what you want; happiness is wanting what you get.

Dale Carnegie

The Prayer of St. Francis of Assisi

Lord, make me an instrument of your peace,
Where there is hatred, let me sow love;
where there is injury, pardon;
where there is doubt, faith;
where there is despair, hope;
where there is darkness, light;
where there is sadness, joy.
O Divine Master,
grant that I may not so much seek to be consoled as to console;
to be understood as to understand;
to be loved as to love.
For it is in giving that we receive;
it is in pardoning that we are pardoned;
and it is in dying that we are born to eternal life.

Goals for February

Efforts and courage are not enough without purpose and direction.

John F. Kennedy

February

Let there be peace on earth, and let it begin with me.

Jill Jackson Miller

FRIDAY 1

Visualize peace; create peace around yourself

SATURDAY 2

The heaviest thing you can carry is a grudge

SUNDAY 3

You lie loudest when you lie to yourself

Love all. Trust a few. Do wrong to no one.
William Shakespeare

When you find peace
within yourself,
you become the
kind of person who
can live at peace
with others.
Pe ace Pilgrim

Live simply that others might simply live.

 February

The smallest act of kindness is worth more than the grandest intention.
Oscar Wilde

MONDAY 4

Make the most of life - it has an expiry date

TUESDAY 5

Clear your workspace

WEDNESDAY 6

Keep busy with enjoyable activities

Gratitude unlocks the fullness of life.
It turns what we have into **enough**, and more.
It turns denial into **acceptance**,
chaos to **order**, confusion to **clarity**.
It can turn a meal into a **feast**,
a house into a **home**, a stranger into a **friend**.
Gratitude makes **sense** of our past,
brings **peace** for today,
and creates a **vision** for tomorrow.
Melody Beattie

THANK YOU

Real generosity to the future lies in giving all to the present. *Albert Camus*

Who are you?

You are strong when you take your grief and teach it to smile

You are happy when you overcome your fear and help others do the same

You are brave when your own pain does not blind you to the pain of others

You are loving when you see a flower and are thankful for the blessing

You are wise when you know the limits of your own wisdom

You are true when you admit there are times when you fool yourself

You are alive when tomorrow's hope means more to you than yesterdays mistake

You are growing when you know what you are but not what you will become

You are free when you are in control of yourself and have no wish to control others

You are honourable when you find your honour is to honour others

You are generous when you can take as sweetly as you give

You are humble when you do not know how humble you are

You are thoughtful when you see me just as I am and treat me just as you are

You are merciful when you forgive in others the faults you condemn in yourself

You are beautiful when you don't need a mirror to tell you.

You are rich when you never need more than what you have

You are you

when you are at peace

with who you are.

Instead of comparing yourself to others,
recognise that you have a uniqueness that makes you beautiful
and a beauty that makes you unique.

February

Find the beauty and adventure in uncertainty and you will be free.

As soon as you trust yourself, you will know how to live.

Johann Wolfgang Goethe

THURSDAY 7

Treasure the mystery and wonder of life

SATURDAY 8

Be clear about your life's purpose

WEDNESDAY 9

Enthusiasm for life reflects positively on your health

SUNDAY 10

Be energy efficient

Speak in a way that others love listening to you and listen in a way that others love speaking to you.

February

Courage is resistance to fear mastery of fear, not absence of fear.
Mark Twain

MONDAY 11

Every thought we think is creating our future

TUESDAY 12

Make time for a 30-minute walk daily

WEDNESDAY 13

Sometimes less is more

The healthiest of all human emotions is gratitude.
Zig Ziglar

The full measure of a man is
not to be found in the man himself,
but in the colours and textures
that come alive in others
because of him.
Albert Schweitzer

You have only one chance to make a good first impression.

 # February

Always remember you are absolutely unique, just like everyone else.
Margaret Mead

THURSDAY 14

Make someone feel good about themselves today

FRIDAY 15

Use your support network

SATURDAY 16

Balance constancy with change

SUNDAY 17

See beauty in the familiar

Being a role model is the most powerful form of educating. Youngsters need good models more than they need critics.
It is one of a parents' greatest responsibilities and opportunities.

If we don't start, it is certain we cannot arrive.

February

The purest ore is produced from the hottest furnace, and the brightest thunderbolt is elicited from the darkest storm.

Charles Cotton

MONDAY 18

Stay true to your life's purpose

TUESDAY 19

True love has no limits and no conditions

WEDNESDAY 20

Be generous with your time

THURSDAY 21

Believe in a higher power

We cannot change anything until we accept it.

I am a wonder woman.
I wonder where I left my keys
I wonder how I put on weight
I wonder where my money goes
I wonder where I put my glasses
I wonder why I wonder ....

Plant, for the Garden of Your Life

. If you plant honesty, you will reap trust.

. If you plant goodness, you will reap friends.

. If you plant humility, you will reap greatness.

. If you plant perseverance, you will reap contentment.

. If you plant consideration, you will reap perspective.

. If you plant hard work, you will reap success.

. If you plant forgiveness, you will reap reconciliation.

First aid for the soul

Be yourself, truthfully

Accept yourself, gratefully

Value yourself, joyfully

Forgive yourself, completely

Treat yourself, generously

Balance yourself, harmoniously

Trust yourself, confidently

Love yourself, wholeheartedly

Empower yourself, immediately

Give yourself, enthusiastically

Express yourself, radiantly

Nourish yourself, responsibly

Often has a ship been lost close to the harbour.

February

You cannot wake a person who is pretending to be asleep

Navajo Proverb

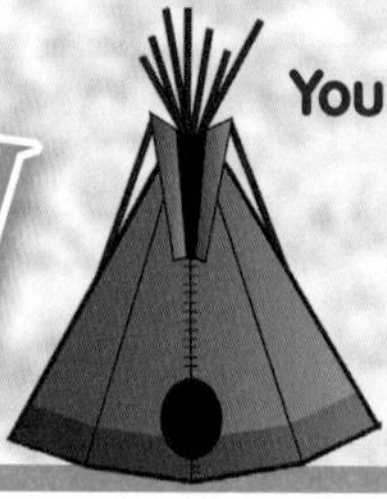

FRIDAY 22

Know that you are never alone

SATURDAY 23

Give up any self-inflicted suffering

SUNDAY 24

Grant others the freedom to be themselves

**If we had no winter,
the spring would not be so pleasant:
if we did not sometimes
taste of adversity,
prosperity would not
be so welcome.**

Anne Bradstreet

However great the flood, it will ebb.

February

**Do not pray for an easier life.
Pray to be a stronger person.**
John F. Kennedy

MONDAY 25

Assumptions limit what's possible

TUESDAY 26

The past is over and done, let it go with love

WEDNESDAY 27

Organise your paper work

THURSDAY 28

Pay your bills with a happy heart

---

*Don't die with your music still inside you.
Listen with your intuitive inner voice and
find what passion stirs your soul.*
Wayne Dyer

**If you want to build a relationship
make trust as your brick and patience as your cement.
Just love is not enough.**

There are only **4** ways in which we connect with the world: what we do, how we look, what we say and how we say it.

Dale Carnagie

Goals for March

Winning isn't everything, but wanting to win is.

Vince Lombardi

If I have been of **service**,

If I have **glimpsed** more of the nature and essence of ultimate God,

If I am **inspired** to reach wider horizons of thought and action,

If I am at **peace** with myself,

It has been a **Successful Day.**

 # March

FRIDAY 1 — St. David's Day

Be clear on what you wish to accomplish

SATURDAY 2

Every day is a new opportunity for a new beginning

SUNDAY 3

Sometimes criticism is constructive

When an archer misses the mark, he turns
and looks for the fault within himself.
Failure to hit the bulls eye is never
the fault of the target.
To improve your aim, improve yourself.
Gilbert Arland.

Understand that the right to
choose your own path
is a sacred privilege.
Use it. Dwell in possibility.
Oprah Winfrey

Those who fear the darkness have no idea what the light can do.

 # March

Life is really simple, but men insist on making it complicated.
Confucious

MONDAY 4

Do the right thing

TUESDAY 5

Smile. Most of what you worry about never happens

WEDNESDAY 6

Look for the silver lining

THURSDAY 7

Be a warrior for quality

The most valuable possession you can own is an open heart.
The most powerful weapon you can be is an instrument of peace.
Carlos Santana

Running away from a problem only increases the distance from any solution.

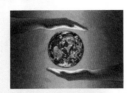

**Universal compassion
is the only guarantee
of morality.**

Arthur Schopenhauer

FRIDAY 8

Work on overcoming your fears

SATURDAY 9

Love others just the way they are

SUNDAY 10

Celebrate Mother's Day

*In life we will realise there is a purpose
for everyone we meet.
Some will test us.
Some will use us,
and some will teach us,
But the most important are the ones
who bring out the best in us, respect us
and accept us for who we are.
Our purpose is to be one of these people.*

**Hope is the little voice that whispers 'maybe' when it
seems the entire world is shouting 'NO'.**

March

Just when the caterpillar thought the world was over, he became a butterfly.

MONDAY 11

Take the world as it comes

TUESDAY 12

Give your best to your work and your relationships

WEDNESDAY 13

Find a new recipe for a healthy meal

THURSDAY 14

We all have a reason for everything

We can let circumstances rule us, or we can take charge and rule our lives from within.

Earl Nightingale

The man who is waiting for something to turn up, might well start with his shirtsleeves.

March

FRIDAY 15

Treasure your loved ones

SATURDAY 16

Take time for the things that matter

Remembered JOY

Don't grieve for me, for now I'm free!
I followed the plan God laid for me.
I saw His face, I heard His call,
I took His hand and left it all...
I could not stay another day,
To love, to laugh, to work or play;
Tasks left undone must stay that way.
And if my parting has left a void,
Then fill it with remembered joy.
A friendship shared, a laugh, a kiss...
Ah yes, these things I, too, shall miss.
My life's been full, I've savoured much:
Good times, good friends, a loved-one's touch.
Perhaps my time seemed all too brief—
Don't shorten yours with undue grief.
Be not burdened with tears of sorrow,
Enjoy the sunshine of the morrow.

Dedicated to the memory of my Aunt Yvonne
Glenda Devlin

March

SUNDAY 17

St. Patrick's Day

Everything in life is temporary

Native Wisdom

A grandfather from the Cherokee Nation
was talking with his grandson.
"A fight is going on inside me" he said to the boy.
It is a terrible fight, and it is between two wolves.
One wolf is evil and ugly; he is anger, envy, greed,
self pity, resentment, selfishness, inferiority, false
pride, lies, guilt, arrogance and war.
The other wolf is beautiful and good; he is friendly,
joyful, generous, peaceful, humble, kind, just,
compassion, forgiveness and gratitude.
The same fight is going on inside you,
and inside every human being.
The grandson paused in deep reflection
on what his grandfather had said.
Then he asked, "Grandfather,
which wolf will win the fight?"
And the Elder replied "the wolf that you feed"

*Men occasionally stumble over the truth, but most of them
pick themselves up, and hurry off as if nothing ever happened*

Winston Churchill

March

**Hide not your talents,
they for use were made.
What's a sundial
in the shade?**

Benjamin Franklin

**There are two primary choices in life:
Choose to accept conditions as they exist or
choose to accept responsibility for changing them.**

MONDAY 18

Even the longest journey begins with the first step

TUESDAY 19

Begin with the end in mind

WEDNESDAY 20

An open mind welcomes an open heart

THURSDAY 21

There is no such thing as a "small" gift

There is an immeasurable distance
between **late** and **too late.**

Og Mandino

Think before you speak, and look before you leap.

 # March

**Use soft words
and hard argument**
English Proverb

FRIDAY 22

Play with your fears

SATURDAY 23

Be bold. Be brave. Be true.

SUNDAY 24

Work towards your highest goals

**Inaction breeds doubt and fear.
Action breeds confidence and courage.
If you want to conquer fear,
do not sit home and think about it.
Go out and get busy.**
Dale Carnegie

 **An ant on the move does
more than a dozing ox.**
Lao Tzu

Desiderata

Go placidly amid the noise and the haste, and remember what peace
there may be in silence. As far as possible, without surrender,
be on good terms with all persons. Speak your truth quietly and clearly;
and listen to others, even to the dull and the ignorant; they too have their story.
Avoid loud and aggressive persons; they are vexatious to the spirit.

If you compare yourself with others, you may become vain or bitter,
for always there will be greater and lesser persons than yourself.
Enjoy your achievements as well as your plans.
Keep interested in your own career, however humble;
it is a real possession in the changing fortunes of time.

Exercise caution in your business affairs, for the world is full of trickery.
But let this not blind you to what virtue there is; many persons strive for
high ideals, and everywhere life is full of heroism. Be yourself.
Especially do not feign affection. Neither be cynical about love,
for in the face of all aridity and disenchantment, it is as perennial as the grass.

Take kindly the counsel of the years, gracefully surrendering the things of youth.
Nurture strength of spirit to shield you in sudden misfortune. But do not distress
yourself with dark imaginings. Many fears are born of fatigue and loneliness.

Beyond a wholesome discipline, be gentle with yourself. You are a child of the universe
no less than the trees and the stars; you have a right to be here.
And whether or not it is clear to you, no doubt the universe is unfolding as it should.

Therefore be at peace with God, whatever you conceive Him to be.
And whatever your labors and aspirations, in the noisy confusion of life,
keep peace in your soul.

With all its sham, drudgery, and broken dreams, it is still a beautiful world.
Be cheerful. Strive to be happy.

Max Ehrmann, Desiderata

March

The mind is not a vessel to be filled, bu a fire to be kindled.
Plutarch

MONDAY 25

Share your heart as deeply as you share your pockets

TUESDAY 26

No one has ever become poor by giving

WEDNESDAY 27

Visualize the future you deserve

THURSDAY 28

Gratitude unlocks the fullness of life

Motherhood has a very humanizing effect.
Everything gets reduced to essentials.
Meryl Streep

Adopt the pace of nature: her secret is patience.
Ralph Waldo Emerson

March

Do, or do not. There is no try.
Yoda

FRIDAY 29

Your contribution is unique, value it

SATURDAY 30

Money often costs too much

SUNDAY 31

Summertime begins today

It's not what you gather, but what you scatter
that tells what kind of life you have lived!

**If your actions inspire others
to dream more, learn more,
do more and become more,
you are a leader.**
John Quincy Adams

We don't see things as they are; we see things as we are.

Goals for April

Nothing can stop the man with the right mental attitude from achieving his goal; Nothing on earth can help the man with the wrong mental attitude.

Thomas Jefferson

Life is like a roll of toilet paper.
The closer it gets to the end,
The faster it goes!

I tried cooking with wine for the first time last night.
After five glasses I forgot why I was in the kitchen!

April

**Outer show is
a poor substitute
for inner worth.**
Aesop

MONDAY 1

Appreciate the beauty of nature

TUESDAY 2

Be gentle with yourself

WEDNESDAY 3

Be grateful for all that you have

THURSDAY 4

Make a dream wish list

What lies behind us and what lies
before us are tiny matters
compared to what lies within us.
Ralph Waldo Emerson

Healthy citizens are the greatest asset any country can have.

 **April**

**Turn your face
to the sun
and the shadows
follow behind you.**
Maori Proverb

FRIDAY 5

Never assume what others might be thinking

SATURDAY 6

Everyone's opinion is valid

SUNDAY 7

Choose your friends

 **life is like a ten speed bicycle
we all have gears we never use.**

So often times it happens, we live our life in the chains we wrought ourselves

**A strong positive mental attitude
will create more miracles than
any wonder drug.**

Patricia Neal

**Those who bring sunshine
to the lives of others
can't keep it
from themselves.**

MONDAY 8

Consider that you are not limited by what you think limits you

TUESDAY 9

Grant yourself freedom

WEDNESDAY 10

Learn and explore

THURSDAY 11

Do something today your future self will thank you for

**To desire and strive to be of some
service to the world.
To aim at doing something
which shall really increase the
happiness, welfare and virtue of mankind
this is a choice which is possible for all of us;
and surely it is a good haven to sail for.**

Henry Van Dyke

Affirmations

I am safe and secure at all times.
I am divinely protected and guided and my way is smooth and easy.
I trust in the process of life to unfold for my highest good and greatest joy.

I allow abundance and prosperity into my life.
I am good enough to have what I want.
I release my negative attitudes which block my experience of pleasure.

I am worthy of my own self love.
There are no failures, I learn from everything I do.
I release judgement and let my life flow.
I am worthy of the very best in life.

I open my heart to love.
I am pure, good, and innocent.
I am confident that the healing power of God's love,
will heal my mind, heart and body.

I am able to harness my will power to control addictive influences in my life
It is safe and right for me to express the best of who I am now.
I will substitute love, joy, and creative expression,
for old problems of addiction and abuse.
I think positive thoughts about my life and everything around me.
I open myself to my intuition and deepest knowing.
I focus on what I love and draw it to me.

I am open and receptive to all life.
I am open to the goodness and abundance of the universe.
I am willing to go beyond my limitations
to express and experience greater joy.

The energy of the mind is the essence of life

Aristotle

April

Sometimes good things fall apart so better things can fall together.

Marilyn Monroe

FRIDAY 12

Be a source of love

SATURDAY 13

Choose the higher road today

SUNDAY 14

Allow yourself to confront your fear of the unknown

Be thankful for those who expect a lot from us,

for they provide opportunities for us to use

the natural talents we have received from God.

No one is useless in this world who lightens the burden of it for anyone else.

Charles Dickens

Neighborhood Street Party

Love your neighbour as you love yourself.

MONDAY 15

Bring peace where there is conflict

TUESDAY 16

Design your own future

WEDNESDAY 17

Trust Yourself

THURSDAY 18

Make your own choices

Embrace the challenge, jump into the effort,
and work your way through the difficulties.
There is great value in the doing, and now is your opportunity
to bring that value to life.
Ralph Marston

Your children need your prescence more than your presents.
Jesse Jackson

April

Don't look back, you're not going that way.

FRIDAY 19

Turn problems into challenges

SATURDAY 20

The secret to a joyful life is acceptance

SUNDAY 21

Consider your obligations

Live... without pretending
Love... without depending
Listen... without defending
Speak... without offending

If you must meddle in human relationships,
try to be a peacemaker.
You will find that you don't have much competition.

Every saint has a past, and every sinner has a future.
Oscar Wilde

You don't get harmony when everybody sings the same note.
Doug Floyd

MONDAY 22

Listen to the sound of silence

TUESDAY 23

Have compassion for your own humanity

WEDNESDAY 24

St George's Day.   Challenge your negative beliefs

Today, I will be the master of my emotions –

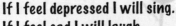

If I feel depressed I will sing.
If I feel sad I will laugh.
If I feel ill I will double my labour.
If I feel fear I will plunge ahead.
If I feel inferior I will wear new garments.
If I feel uncertain I will raise my voice.
If I feel poverty I will think of wealth to come.
If I feel incompetent I will think of past success.
If I feel insignificant I will remember my goals.
Today I will be the master of my emotions.

Og Mandino

Knowing others is intelligence; knowing yourself is true wisdom
Mastering others is strength; mastering yourself is true power

Lao Tzu

April

To fall in love is awfully simple, but to fall out of love is simply awful.

Bess Myerson

THURSDAY 25

Be the one who makes the difference

FRIDAY 26

You are worthy of love

SATURDAY 27

Say 'yes' or 'no' and move on

SUNDAY 28

Learn to enjoy your own company

A wise old owl lived in an oak.
The more he saw
The less he spoke.
The less he spoke
The more he heard.
Why can't I be
like that wise old bird?

Don't be pushed by your problems, be pulled by your dreams.

April

Walking is man's best medicine.

Hippocrates

MONDAY 29

A helping hand is worth more than good advice

TUESDAY 30

Letting go doesn't mean giving up

Goals for May

If you don't know where you are going, any road will get you there.

Lewis Carroll

 **May**

**Never greet the dawn
without a map.**

WEDNESDAY 1

Find value in the doing

THURSDAY 2

There are no small acts of kindness

FRIDAY 3

If you can't see the bright side of life, polish up the dull side

SATURDAY 4

Refuse to listen to your own excuses

SUNDAY 5

Keep your standards high

*If you are stopped by fear, the world is deprived of your
contribution, and you are deprived of an experience of being alive.*

May

**Bread for myself
is a material question.
Bread for my neighbour
is a spiritual one.**

Nikolai Berdyae

MONDAY 6

True passion comes from true purpose

TUESDAY 7

Look beyond your narrow concerns

WEDNESDAY 8

The best of life's possibilities are here right now

THURSDAY 9

Any choice you make is a turn your life takes

When you are sorrowful look again in your heart,
and you shall see that, in truth, you are weeping
for that which has been your delight.

Kahlil Gibran

**Choose to see the world through grateful eyes;
it will never look the same again.**

It's okay to burn the biscuits!

When I was a kid, my mum liked to make breakfast food for dinner every now and then. And I remember one night in particular when she had made dinner after a long, hard day at work. On that evening so long ago, my mum placed a plate of eggs and sausage, and extremely burned biscuits in front of my dad. I remember waiting to see if anyone noticed! Yet all my dad did was reach for his Biscuit, smile at my mum and ask me how my day was at school.

I don't remember what I told him that night, but I do remember hearing my mum apologize to my dad for burning the biscuits. And I'll never forget what he said: "Honey, I love burned biscuits."

Later that night, I went to kiss Daddy good night and I asked him if he really liked his biscuits burned. He wrapped me in his arms and said, "Your mummy put in a long hard day at work today and she's really tired. And besides... a burnt biscuit never hurt anyone!"

You know, life is full of imperfect things... and imperfect people. I'm not the best at hardly anything, and I forget birthdays and anniversaries just like everyone else. What I've learned over the years is that learning to accept each others faults and choosing to celebrate each others differences, is one of the most important keys to creating a healthy, growing, and lasting relationship.

So......please pass me a biscuit. And yes, the burned one will do just fine!

Don't put the key to you happiness in someone else's pocket, keep it in your own.

May

Trust is the foundation of any worthwhile relationship.

FRIDAY 10

Clear out the clutter

SATURDAY 11

Get busy outdoors

SUNDAY 12

Life is not just about getting by

The more generous we are, the more joyous we become.

The more cooperative we are, the more valuable we become.

The more enthusiastic we are, the more productive we become.

The more serving we are, the more prosperous we become.

William Arthur War

Death leaves a heartache
no one can heal.
Love leaves a memory
no one can steal.

May

The body heals with play
The mind heals with laughter
The spirit heals with joy.

Proverb

MONDAY 13

Share the love that lives within you

TUESDAY 14

Direct your energy into the things that truly matter

WEDNESDAY 15

The more you think you are, the more you are

THURSDAY 16

Right now, you have great power to do great things

Always remember to forget
the troubles that passed away;
But never forget to remember
the blessings that come each day.

Talk to yourself they way you would talk to someone you love.

May

Education is not filling a bucket, but lighting a fire.
WB Yeats

If you don't act now, while it is fresh in your mind, it will probably join the list of things you were always going to do, but never quite got round to. Chances are, you'll also miss some opportunities.
Paul Clithero

FRIDAY 17

Be your very best you today

SATURDAY 18

Don't weigh yourself down with judgments

SUNDAY 19

Plan for success

A person without a sense of humour
is like a wagon without springs.
It's jolted by every pebble on the road.
Henry Ward Beecher

To love is to recognise yourself in another.
Eckart Tolle

The αbets dare:

Dare to:

Ask for what you want, **B**elieve in miracles,
Change your mind, **D**o the impossible,
Embrace abundance, **F**ollow your hearts desire,
Grow and unfold, **H**arvest your dreams,
Impress yourself, **J**ust say yes, **K**iss and make up,
Love and be loved, **M**ake mistakes, **N**urture your spirit,
Overcome adversity, **P**lay more, **Q**uestion beliefs,
Reach for the stars, **S**peak your truth,
Take responsibility, **U**nderstand who you are,
Volunteer your time, **W**alk through fear,
Xperience the moment, **Y**earn for grace,
take every opportunity to be **Z**any.

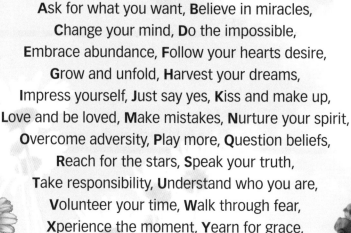

I am tomorrow, or some future day,
what I establish today.
I am today, what I established yesterday
or some previous day.

James Joyce

Take time to laugh.........................It is the music of the soul.

Take time to think. ....It is the source of power.

Take time to play. ....It is the source of perpetual youth.

Take time to read. ....It is the fountain of wisdom.

Take time to pray. ....It is the greatest power on Earth.

Take time to love and be loved. ....It is a God-given privilege.

Take time to be friendly. ....It is the road to happiness.

Take time to give. ....It is too short a day to be selfish.

Take time to work. ....It is the price of success.

Take time to deliberate,
but when the time
for action has arrived,
stop thinking and go.

MONDAY 20

Don't be held back by the momentum of idleness

TUESDAY 21

Life is filled with endless opportunities

WEDNESDAY 22

Achievement is built on challenge

THURSDAY 23

Be curious, not judgemental

3 simple rules in life:

1) If you don't go after what you want, you'll never have it.

2) If you do not ask, the answer will always be 'no'.

3) If you do not step forward, you will always be in the same place.

Do It Anyway

People are often unreasonable, illogical and self-centered;
Forgive them anyway.

If you are kind, people may accuse you of selfish ulterior motives;
Be kind anyway.

If you are successful,
you will win some false friends and true enemies;
Succeed anyway.

If you are honest and frank, people may cheat you;
Be honest anyway.

What you spend years building, someone could destroy overnight;
Build anyway.

If you find serenity and happiness, they may be jealous;
Be happy anyway.

The good you do today, people will often forget tomorrow;
Do good anyway.

Give the world the best you have, and it may never be enough;
Give the world the best you've got anyway.

You see, in the final analysis, it is between you and God;
It was never between you and them anyway.

Mother Teresa.

To be kind is more important than to be right.
Many times what people need
is not a brilliant mind that speaks,
but a special heart that listens.

May

Why are you trying to fit in when you were born to stand out?

FRIDAY 24

Acknowledge the gifts in your life

SATURDAY 25

Spend time with enthusastic people

SUNDAY 26

Be yourself. Be kind. Be cause.

To understand the heart and mind of a person, look not only at what he has already achieved, but also look at what he aspires to.

I never considered a difference of opinion in politics, in religion, in philosophy, as cause for withdrawing from a friend.

Thomas Jefferson

Success is the ability to go from one failure to another with no loss of enthusiasm

Winston Churchhill

May

"Rock bottom became the solid foundation on which I rebuilt my life."
JK Rowling

MONDAY 27

Stop, look around, breathe, be grateful for everything

TUESDAY 28

Write a letter to someone you love

WEDNESDAY 29

Fear is nothing more than a state of mind

THURSDAY 30

Have a 'fruit and veg' day

Most of us miss out on life's big prizes…Pulitzer, Nobel, Oscars, The World Cup…. But we're all eligible for life's smaller prizes…
A pat on the back. A kiss behind the ear.
A full moon. An empty parking space.
A crackling fire. A great meal. A glorious sunset.
Hot soup. Cold beer. A hot shower. A comfortable bed.

The best way to predict the future is to create it.
Peter F. Drucker

May

We are called
to be the architects
of the future,
not its victims.

R. Buckminster Fuller

FRIDAY 31

Plan a new venture

Goals for June

If a man does not know what port he is steering for,
no wind is favourable to him.

Seneca

We have to grow from the inside out. No one can teach us.
No one can make us spiritual. There is no other teacher but our own soul.

Vivekenanda

June

**Deal with the faults
of others
as gently as with
your own.**
Chinese proverb

SATURDAY 1

Treasure every moment you have on this earth

SUNDAY 2

You will never regret being kind

**A man's mind stretched by new
ideas can never go back to its
original dimensions.**

(Oliver Wendell Holmes)

The person who sows a single beautiful thought
in the mind of another, renders the world
a greater service than that rendered
by all the faultfinders combined .
Napoleon Hill

Any fool can criticize, and many fools do.
Dale Carnegie

 **June**

**Life doesn't come
with a remote control;
you have to get up
and change it yourself.**

 To be a star you must shine your own light,
follow your own path,and not worry about
the darkness, for that is when the star shines.

MONDAY 3

Don't settle for less than you deserve

TUESDAY 4

Be patient. Give time time

WEDNESDAY 5

You are as powerful and strong as you allow yourself to be

THURSDAY 6

Engage in life long learning

**The most important thing is not to stop questioning.
Curiosity has its own reason for existing.**

Albert Einstein

After a while you learn

the subtle difference between holding a hand and chaining a soul.
And you learn that love doesn't mean possession,
and company doesn't mean security.
And you begin to learn that kisses aren't contracts,
and presents aren't promises.
And you begin to accept your defeats with your head up
and your eyes ahead,
with the grace of an adult, not the grief of a child.
And you learn to build your roads on today,
because tomorrows ground is too uncertain for plans,
and futures have a way of falling down in mid flight.
After a while you learn
that even sunshine burns if you get too much.
So you plant your own garden, and decorate your own soul,
instead of waiting for someone to bring you flowers.
And you learn that you really can endure, that you really are strong,
and you really do have worth,
And you learn, and you learn, and you learn...

Veronica A Shoffstall

One day at a time is enough
Don't look back and grieve the past,
it is gone.
Don't be troubled about the future,
it has yet to come.
Live in the present moment,
and make it so beautiful
It will be worth remembering.

Go for it now, the future is promised to no one.

 June

**Blessed are the cracked,
for they let in the light.**

FRIDAY 7

Don't expect others to be like you

SATURDAY 8

Spend quality time with your children and pets

SUNDAY 9

Find the perfect picnic place

If you want to awaken all of humanity then awaken all of yourself
If you want to eliminate the suffering in the world,
then eliminate all that is dark and negative in yourself.
Truly the greatest gift you have to give, is that of your own self transformation.
Lao Tzu

Be content with what you have.
Rejoice in the way things are.
When you realise there is nothing lacking
the whole world belongs to you.

I don't think of the past. The only thing that matters is the everlasting presen
W. Somerset Maugham

 **June**

**Imagination is everything;
it is the preview of
life's coming attractions.**
Albert Einstein

MONDAY 10

Never allow one dispute to injure a friendship

TUESDAY 11

You cannot re-live time

WEDNESDAY 12

Happiness comes from within

A friend is one who knows you as you are,

understands where you've been,

accepts who you've become,

and still gently invites you to grow.

*The weak cannot forgive.
Forgiveness is an attribute of the strong.*

Mahatma Gandhi

June

The future belongs to those who believe in the beauty of their dreams.
Eleanor Roosevelt

THURSDAY 13

The best things in life are free

FRIDAY 14

However good or bad a situation is, it will change

SATURDAY 15

Notice what you eat and read

SUNDAY 16

Celebrate Father's Day

My mission in life is not merely to
survive, but to thrive;
and to do so with some passion,
some compassion,
some humour
and some style.
Maya Angelou

Fears are nothin More Than A State Of Mind

Your feet will take you to where your heart wants to go.

Be Someone

Be someone who **listens**, you will be **heard**.

Be someone who **cares**, you will be **loved**.

Be someone who **gives**, you will be **blessed**.

Be someone who **comforts** you will know **peace**.

Be someone who seeks to **understand**, you will be **wise**.

Be someone who **loves**, you will be **happy**.

Be someone who values **truth**, you will be **respected**.

Be someone who takes **action**, you will move life **forward**.

Be someone who lifts others **higher**, your life will be **rich**.

Be someone filled with **gratitude**, and there will be no **end**

to the things for **which** you will be **thankful**.

Be someone who **lives** with **joy** and **purpose**

and your own **light** will brightly **shine**.

Be in every moment the **special** someone you are meant to be...

Be Yourself

Those who fear the darkness
Have no idea what the light can do.

If you want to understand yourself -
look into the hearts of other people.
If you want to understand other people -
look into your own heart.

The only disability in life is a bad attitude.

June

**If you mess up
'Fess up!**

MONDAY 17

Accept good advice when you get it

TUESDAY 18

Say YES to the longings of your own heart

WEDNESDAY 19

You are as important as anyone else

THURSDAY 20

Be grateful that you are you

**How blissful our lives are when
we know what is deeply important to us.
With this picture in mind, it is easy to manage
ourselves each day, to be, and to do,
what really matters most to us.**

Life and time are the world's best teachers.

June

**Be a good listener.
Your ears will
never get you
into trouble.**

FRIDAY 21

Consider the difference between want and need

SATURDAY 22

Wipe the slate clean - erase all your regrets

SUNDAY 23

The struggle ends when the gratitude begins

All in the dark we grope along,
And if we go amiss
We learn at least which path is wrong,
And there is gain in this.
We do not always win the race
By only running right;
We have to tread the mountain's base
Before we reach its height.

Ella Wheeler Wilcox

Praise youth and it will prosper.
Irish proverb

June

MONDAY 24

Have the courage to admit when you're wrong

TUESDAY 25

Get rid of anything that isn't useful, beautiful or joyful

WEDNESDAY 26

Be eccentric now. Don't wait for old age to wear purple

Through humour,
you can soften
some of the worst blows
that life delivers.
And once you find laughter,
no matter how painful
your situation might be,
you can survive it.
Bill Cosby

Don't let anyone else take the measure of your worth and capabilities.

Margaret Spellings

THURSDAY 27

Over prepare, then go with the flow

FRIDAY 28

Whatever doesn't kill you really does make you stronger

SATURDAY 29

Everything can change in the blink of an eye

SUNDAY 30

Be open to new ideas

Mans search for meaning....

We who lived in concentration camps can remember the men who walked through the huts, comforting others, giving away their last piece of bread.
They may have been few in number, but they offer sufficient proof, that everything can be taken from a man, but one thing, the last of the human freedoms - to choose ones' attitude in any given set of circumstances; to choose ones' own way."

Victor Frankl

Those who take instruction will prosper

Goals for July

Opportunity is missed by most people because it is dresses in overalls and looks like work.

Thomas A. Edison

MONDAY 1

Do not knowingly cause upset

You are the only one that creates your own reality.

**Time cools, time clarifies;
no mood can be maintained
quite unaltered
through the course of hours.**
Mark Twain

What may be done at any time, will be done at no time.
Scottish Proverb

TUESDAY 2

Think outside of the box

WEDNESDAY 3

No one is in charge of your happiness but you

THURSDAY 4

Who we are is what we speak

*The bitterest tears shed over graves
are for words left unsaid
and deeds left undone.*

Harriet Beecher Stowe

**If you want peace, stop fighting,
If you want peace of mind, stop fighting with your thoughts.**

Peter McWilliams

FRIDAY 5

Everyone's opinion is valid

SATURDAY 6

This is how it turns out

SUNDAY 7

There is no 'no' in Life

Wishes and blessings

May today there be peace within.
May you trust your highest power
that you are exactly where you are meant to be.
May you not forget the infinite possibilities
that are born of faith.
May you use those gifts that you have received,
and pass on the love that has been given to you.
May you be content knowing you are a child of God.
Let this presence settle into your bones,
and allow your soul the freedom
to sing, dance, and to bask in the sun.
It is there for each and every one of you.

St Teresa's Prayer

**Where will we meet,
given our differences?**

**Out there, beyond ideas
of wrongdoing,
and rightdoing,
there is a field.
I will meet you there.**
Rumi

The Secret Place

*On the water
ancient love glides
forever bound in grace
side by side
silent and easy
no often touch required
direction certain and
understood.
A life devoted
we like the swans
blessed.*
(B. Devlin)

Nothing is a waste of time if you use the experience wisely.
Rodin

July

The world hates change, yet it is the only thing that has brought progress.

Charles Kettering

MONDAY 8

Be responsible for what you do and what you say

TUESDAY 9

Grant yourself permission to be your true self

WEDNESDAY 10

Bring peace into moments of chaos

THURSDAY 11

The only person you can change is yourself

The world would be a different place if we all could just slow down enough to consider what is true and real . . . and always try to understand how other people feel. The place to start is with ourselves.

Time is the most valuable thing you can spend.

July

An apology is the super glue of life. It can repair just about anything.
Lynn Johnston

FRIDAY 12

Worry less and dream more

SATURDAY 13

Communicate clearly

Self discipline begins with Mastery of your own thoughts. If you don't control what you think, You can't control what you say or do.

Knowing is not enough, We must apply Willing is not enough, We must do.
Johann Wolfgang von Goethe

Worrying is like sitting in a rocking chair
- it gives you something to do
but it doesn't get you anywhere.

There are no limitations to the mind except those we acknowledge.

July

Change brings new gifts, if we are ready to accept them.

Simplicity is the ultimate sophistication.

SUNDAY 14

Be grateful for happy memories

> Friends are helpful
> not only because
> they will listen to us,
> but because they
> will laugh at us;
> Through them we learn
> a little objectivity,
> a little modesty,
> a little courtesy;
> We learn the rules of life
> and become better
> players of the game.
> *Will Durant*

Student says: I am very discouraged. What should I do?
Master says: Encourage others.

**You never know how
strong you are,
until being strong is
your only choice.**

MONDAY 15

When in doubt, just take the next small step

TUESDAY 16

Life isn't fair, but it's still good

WEDNESDAY 17

Don't take yourself so seriously. No one else does

THURSDAY 18

Be of service to those who are less fortunate than yourself

Don't compare your life to others;
you have no idea what their journey is all about.

**At least once in your lifetime, you meet
a person who leaves an impression on your
soul that time will never erase.**

July

The secret to staying young is to live honestly, eat slowly and lie about your age!
Lucille Ball

Motivation is what gets you started. Habit is what keeps you going.

FRIDAY 19

Be a good role model

SATURDAY 20

Give someone the gift your time

SUNDAY 21

Listen. Listen. Listen

**Life is a roller coaster -
you can either scream every time you hit a bump,
or you can throw your hands up in the air
and enjoy the ride.**

**Where there is shouting
there is no true knowledge.**

Leonardo de Vinci

Dust if you must.
But wouldn't it be better, to paint a picture, or write a letter,
Bake a cake, or plant a seed,
Ponder the difference between want and need?

Dust if you must.
But there is not much time
With rivers to swim and mountains to climb!
Music to hear, and books to read,
Friends to cherish and life to lead.

Dust if you must.
But the world's out there
With the sun in your eyes, the wind in your hair,
A flutter of snow, a shower of rain.
This day will not come round again.

Dust if you must.
But bear in mind, old age will come and it's not kind.
And when you go, and go you must,
You, yourself, will make more dust.

Rose Milligan

Find a way to be thankful for your troubles,
and they can become your blessings.

Thank You!

To live by choice, not by chance.
To make changes, not excuses.
To be motivated, not manipulated.
To be useful, not used.
To excel, not compete.
Self esteem, not self pity.
To listen to my inner voice,
not the random opinion of others.

# July

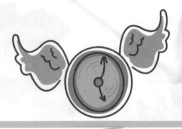

**Time is at once
the most valuable
and the most perishable
of all our possessions.**
John Randolph

MONDAY 22

Be caring and gracious

TUESDAY 23

Price is what you pay. Value is what you get

WEDNESDAY 24

Use the power of your imagination

Finish each day and be done with it.
You have done what you could;
some blunders and absurdities have crept in;
forget them as soon as you can.
Tomorrow is a new day;
you shall begin it serenely
and with too high a spirit
to be encumbered with your old nonsense.
Ralph Waldo Emerson

If we take care of the moments, the years will take care of themselves.

July

**The truth is the truth,
even if no one believes it.
A lie is a lie
even if every one believes it.**

THURSDAY 25

Give someone a pleasant surprise

FRIDAY 26

Invite a neighbour for dinner

SATURDAY 27

Act as if it were impossible to fail

SUNDAY 28

Be open to another point of view

**Action is a great restorer and builder of confidence.
Inaction is not only the result, but the cause, of fear.
Perhaps the action you take will be successful;
Perhaps different action or adjustments
will have to follow.
But any action is better than no action at all.**

Norman Vincent Peale

What worries you, masters you.

 July

It always seems impossible until its done.
Nelson Mandela

MONDAY 29

Be content with less

TUESDAY 30

Think kindly of someone who is struggling

WEDNESDAY 31

Differences enrich families

Goals for August

What you get by achieving your goals is not as important as who you become by achieving your goals.
Henry David Thoreau

August

The best way to succeed in this world is to act on the advice you give to others.

THURSDAY 1

Enjoy the outdoors

FRIDAY 2

Visualize your end result as having already been accomplished

SATURDAY 3

Balance activity with serenity

SUNDAY 4

Tidy your clothes cupboards

All truths are easy to understand once they are discovered; The point is to discover them.
Galileo Galilei

Nothing is as far away as one minute ago.

This is the true joy in life,
being used for a purpose
recognized by yourself as a mighty one.
Being a force of nature
instead of a feverish, selfish
little clod of ailments and grievances
complaining that the world will not
devote itself to making you happy.
I am of the opinion
that my life belongs
to the whole community
and as I live it is my privilege –
my privilege to do for it whatever I can.
I want to be thoroughly used up when I die,
for the harder I work the more I love.
I rejoice in life for its own sake.
Life is no brief candle to me;
it is a sort of splendid torch
which I've got a hold of for the moment
and I want to make it burn as brightly as possible
before handing it on
to future generations.

George Bernard Shaw

August

Abundance is not something we acquire; it is something we tune into.
Wayne Dyer

MONDAY 5

Take pleasure in the beauty of the earth

TUESDAY 6

Speak your love. Speak it again. Speak it still once more

WEDNESDAY 7

Gladden the heart of a child

THURSDAY 8

Manifest your loyalty in word and deed

**If you are depressed, you are living in the past.
If you are anxious, you are living in the future.
If you are at peace, you are living in the present.**
Lao Tzu

**If there is something
you've always wanted
to do – Get Up And Go
and Do It Now!**

FRIDAY 9

Share some treasure

SATURDAY 10

Dismiss suspicion and replace it with trust

SUNDAY 11

Make this a day to remember

Sometimes we have to run
away from the people we love,
not because we want them to realise our worth,
but for us to realise our own worth.

*When people walk away from you, let them go.
Your destiny is never tied to anyone who 'leaves' you;
and it doesn't mean they are bad people;
it just means that their part in your journey is complete.*

Most of the shadows of life are caused by us standing in our own sunshine.

Ralph Waldo Emerson

MONDAY 12

Do not participate in gossip

TUESDAY 13

Be an inspiration to others

WEDNESDAY 14

Write a long letter to a dear friend

THURSDAY 15

Do unto others as you would have others do unto you

Don't let the past dictate the future. You own the future, the past owns itself, and you are greater than them both.

Carly Cermak

To sacrifice what you are, to live without belief, that is a fate more terrible than dying. *Joan of Arc*

The Man in the Glass

When you get what you want in your struggle for self
And the world makes you king for a day,
Just go to a mirror and look at yourself,
And see what that man has to say.
For it isn't your father or mother or wife,
Who judgment upon you must pass;
The fellow whose verdict counts most in your life
Is the one starring back from the glass.
He's the fellow to please, never mind all the rest.
For he's with you clear up to the end,
And you've passed the most dangerous, difficult test
If the man in the glass is your friend.
You may be like Jack Horner and "chisel" a plum,
And think you're a wonderful guy,
But the man in the glass says you're only a bum
If you can't look him straight in the eye.
You may fool the whole world down the pathway of years.
And get pats on the back as you pass,
But your final reward will be the heartaches and tears
If you've cheated the man in the glass.

Dale Wimbrow

The strongest Oak in the forest is not the one protected
from the storm and hidden from the sun.

 **August**

FRIDAY 16

Consider things from every angle

SATURDAY 17

Hold on to your dreams

SUNDAY 18

Ignore those who try to discourage you

The Secret
of making dreams come true can be summarized in four C's. They are:

**Curiosity,
Confidence,
Courage and
Constancy**

and the greatest of these is

Confidence.

Walt Disney

Children are curious
and are risk takers.
They have lots of courage.
They venture out into a world
that is immense and dangerous.
A child initially trusts life,
and the processes of life.

John Bradshaw

n case your worried about what's going to become of the younger generation; it's going to grow up and worry about the younger generation.

 # August

What ought not to be done, do not even think of doing.

Epictetus

MONDAY 19

Inspire yourself with your resilience

TUESDAY 20

Enjoy life today, yesterday is gone

WEDNESDAY 21

Family and friends are hidden treasures

THURSDAY 22

Give more than is expected of you

I know that you believe you understood what you think I said, but I'm not sure you realise that what you heard is not what I meant!

Speak quietly and kindly. Be not forward with opinions or advice. If you talk much, this will make you deaf to what others say, and you should know that there are few so wise that they cannot learn from others. *Dhammavadaka*

Love doesn't make the world go round. Love is what makes the ride worthwhile.

Franklin P. Jones

FRIDAY 23

Speak your truth

SATURDAY 24

Encourage youth

SUNDAY 25

Keep your promises

Work for a cause, not for applause
Live life to express, not impress.
Don't strive to make your presence noticed,
Just make your absence felt.

**Don't get tired of doing little things for others.
Sometimes those little things occupy the biggest part of their hearts.**

August

Concern yourself not with what you tried and failed in but with what it is still possible for you to do.
Pope John XXIII

MONDAY 26

Love life first and foremost

TUESDAY 27

Open your eyes and see things as they really are

WEDNESDAY 28

Be honourable in all your dealings

THURSDAY 29

Make it happen

The world is perfect. It's a mess.
It has always been a mess. We are not going to change it.
Our job is to straighten out our own lives.
Joseph Campbell

*At my age I've seen it all, I've heard it all,
I've done it all, I just cant remember it all.*

On the Road of Life

There's a story of the traveller who comes to a
new city and is greeted at the gate.

The traveller asks:

"What are the people like in your city?"

The gatekeeper replies,

"What are the people like in the city you left?"

Traveller: "The people there are all selfish and mean
and are only for themselves."

Gatekeeper: "And that is the kind of people
you will find here as well."

The traveller moved on, and soon another traveller approaches the

Gatekeeper and asks: "What are the people like in your city?"

Gatekeeper: "Tell me about the people in the city that you have left."

Traveller: "Well, the people are kind and giving and
make the very best kind of friends."

Gatekeeper: "And those are the kind of people
you will find in this city as well."

It's a law of Life: We pretty much get what we give.

If you want something, give it first, and it will be returned to you.

Rephrase the Stories of Your Life:

Your Mistakes made way for New Discoveries

Your Conflicts were Opportunities for Growth

Your Upsets were a Source of Wisdom

Your Failures were Turning Points in your life

Your Anger and Resentments became Lessons in Forgiveness

Your Endings were actually Beginnings

Your Ex boyfriends were indeed your Teachers!

You grow up the day you have your first, real laugh.....at yourself!

 **August**

There is no
snooze button
on a cat
who wants breakfast.

FRIDAY 30

You are a unique creation, nothing can replace you

SATURDAY 31

Zero in on your target and go for it!

Goals for September

You can't realize your dreams unless you
have one to begin with..

Thomas A. Edison

September

SUNDAY 1

Practice makes perfect

You are not your height, nor are you the width of your waist. You are not your hair colour, your skin colour, nor are you a shade of lipstick. Your shoe size is of no consequence. You are not defined by the amount of attention you get from males, females or any combination thereof. You are not the number of sit ups you can do, nor are you the number of calories in a day. You are not your car, your job, nor the amount of money you have in the bank. You are no amalgam of these things.

You are the content of your character, you are the ambitions that drive you, you are the goals that you set, you are the things that you laugh at and the words that you say. You are the thoughts that you think and the things that you wonder. You are beautiful and desirable not for the clique you attend, but for the spark of life within you that compels you to make your life a full and meaningful one. You are beautiful not for the shape of the vessel, but for the volume of the soul it carries.

Never explain; your friends don't need it and your enemies wont believe it anyway
Elbert Hubbard

September

MONDAY 2

Be open to the abundance of the universe

TUESDAY 3

When you speak to a person look into their eyes

WEDNESDAY 4

Life is a game of chance. Play to win

THURSDAY 5

Return what you borrow

Opportunity is always knocking. The problem is
that most people have the 'self-doubt' station
in their head turned up way too loud to hear it.
Brian Vaszily

The doorway to success swings outwards, not inwards.

September ??

FRIDAY 6

Good character is above everything else

SATURDAY 7

Secrets are not empowering

SUNDAY 8

Live up to your agreements

Vision without action is a dream. Action without vision is just passing the time. Action with vision is inspiring and causes miracles.

No one is so old as those who have outlived enthusiasm.

Henry David Thoreau

Do you know what happens when you give a procrastinator a good idea?   Nothing.

September

The shell must break before the bird can fly.

MONDAY 9

Be your own hero

TUESDAY 10

Showing consideration to others, is honouring yourself

WEDNESDAY 11

Live within your means, or expand your means

THURSDAY 12

Resist justifying yourself

The old believe everything, The middle-aged suspect everything, The young know everything.

Oscar Wilde

We have flown the air like birds, and swum the sea like fishes, but we have yet to learn the simple act of walking the earth like brothers.

Martin Luther King Jnr

September

FRIDAY 13

Love is a universal force that permeates everything

SATURDAY 14

Deal calmly with emotional turbulence

SUNDAY 15

Revealing your vulnerability creates intimacy

Don't let someone who gave up on their dreams
talk you out of going after yours.

Try a thing you haven't done, three times.
Once, to get over the fear of doing it.
Twice, to learn how to do it.
And a third time, to figure out
whether you like it or not.

Virgil Garnett Thomson

The opinion others have of you, is their business, not yours.

September

MONDAY 16

Free yourself from anger and self-pity

TUESDAY 17

If you fear something, just go and do it

WEDNESDAY 18

Mend a quarrel

THURSDAY 19

Thank a friend for being your friend

September

You can do anything, but not everything.
David Allen

FRIDAY 20

Balance diet and exercise for a healthy weight

SATURDAY 21

Develop an enthusiastic attitude

SUNDAY 22

Do what inspires you

If a fellow isn't thankful for what he's got,
he's unlikely to be thankful for what he's going to get.

Courage is not the absence of fear,
but rather the judgement
that something else
is more important than fear.
Ambrose Redmoon

It is better to be out of money, than to be out of
creative new ideas on how to make money.

A Creed To Live By

Don't undermine your worth by
comparing yourself with others;
it is because we are different that each of us is special.
Don't set your goals by what other people deem important;
only you know what is best for you.
Don't take for granted the things closest to your heart;
cling to them as you would your life, for without them life is meaningless
Don't let your life slip through your fingers by living
in the past or for the future;
by living your life one day at a time, you live all the days of your life.
Don't give up when you still have something to give;
nothing is really over until the moment you stop trying.
Don't be afraid to admit that you are less than perfect,
it is this fragile thread that binds us to each other.
Don't be afraid to encounter risks;
it is by taking chances that we learn how to be brave.
Don't shut love out of your life by saying it's impossible to find;
the quickest way to receive love is to give love.
The fastest way to lose love is to hold it too tightly;
and the best way to keep love is to give it wings.
Don't dismiss your dreams;
to be without dreams is to be without hope;
to be without hope is to be without purpose.
Don't run through life so fast that you forget
not only where you've been,
but also where you're going.
Life is not a race,
but a journey to be savoured
each step of the way.

Nancye Sims

September

The source of happiness is freedom, and the source of freedom is courage.

MONDAY 23

Surround yourself with creative people

TUESDAY 24

Rest when you are tired

WEDNESDAY 25

Take control of your own destiny

THURSDAY 26

Keep your car clean

tand up or what ou believe , even if : means tanding lone.

You and I possess within ourselves, at every moment of our lives, under all circumstances, the power to transform the quality of our lives.
Werner Erhard

September

We may not hav
it all together,
but together
we have it all!

FRIDAY 27

Laugh and the world laughs with you

SATURDAY 28

Happiness is a state, not a circumstance

SUNDAY 29

Make time for new things

Don't waste time learning the
"tricks of the trade."
Instead, learn the trade.

Strength does not come from winning.
Your struggles develop your strengths.
When you go through hardships
and decide not to surrender,
that is strength.

Mahatma Gandhi

Quitters never win and winners never quit

September

Thinking will not overcome fear but action will.

MONDAY 30

Allow yourself to make mistakes

Goals for October

The tragedy of life doesn't lie in not reaching a goal, the tragedy lies in having no goal to reach.
Thomas A. Edison

Trust yourself
Create the kind of self that you will be happy to live with all your life.
Make the most of yourself by fanning the tiny inner sparks of possibility into flames of achievement. *Golda Meir*

October

**Remember,
no matter where you go,
you take yourself with you.**

TUESDAY 1

Failure is always temporary, giving up makes it permanent

WEDNESDAY 2

Do a little more every day than you think you can

THURSDAY 3

Start a new habit

To dream anything that you want to dream,
that's the beauty of the human mind.
To do anything that you want to do,
that's the strength of the human will.
To trust yourself to test your limits,
that's the courage of the human heart.

Those who are lifting the world
upward and onward are those who
encourage more than criticize.

Elizabeth Harrison

October

We must bring
our own light
to the darkness.

FRIDAY 4

Be generous

SATURDAY 5

There is merit in new ideas and old wisdom

SUNDAY 6

Trust yourself to trust others

our time is limited, so don't waste it living
omeone else's life. Don't be trapped by dogma
which is living with the results of other peoples
hinking. Don't let the noise of other people
hinking drown out your own voice. And most
nportant, have the courage to follow your heart
nd intuition. They already know what you truly
vant to become. Everything else is secondary.

Steve Jobs

*If you don't like something, change it,
if you can't change it, change the way you think about it.*

October

Appreciation can make a
day, even change a life.
Your willingness to put
it into words is all
that is necessary.

Margaret Cousins

MONDAY 7

Be confident in your abilities

TUESDAY 8

Eat less, exercise more

WEDNESDAY 9

Practice contentment

THURSDAY 10

Love unconditionally

At times our own light goes out and
is rekindled by a spark from another person.
Each of us has cause to think with deep gratitude of those
who have lighted the flame within us.   *Albert Schweitzer*

Compassion is a balm for many wounds.

October

**Search others
for their virtues,
thyself for thy vices.**
Benjamin Franklin

FRIDAY 11

The only adult you are responsible for is yourself

SATURDAY 12

Be satisfied with what you have

SUNDAY 13

Listen to new music

B 4

Before you speak, listen.
Before you write, think.
Before you spend, earn.
Before you invest, investigate.
Before you criticize, wait.
Before you pray, forgive.
Before you quit, try.
Before you retire, save.
Before you die, give.
William Arthur Ward

*It is easier to be wise
for others then for
ourselves.*

Treasure silence when you find it.

October

MONDAY 14

Be a seeker of knowledge and wisdom

TUESDAY 15

Make an appointment to have a health check up

WEDNESDAY 16

Imagine life without regrets

THURSDAY 17

Think win-win

**What we think, we become.
All that we are arises with our thoughts.
With our thoughts, we make the world.**

In times like these it helps to recall that there have always been times like these .
Paul Harvey

October

**To a child,
love is spelled
T-I-M-E.**

FRIDAY 18

Talk it over with someone you trust

SATURDAY 19

Self expression is essential to life

SUNDAY 20

Don't leave until tomorrow what can be done today

**"Around here, we don't look
backwards for very long.
We keep moving forwards,
opening up new doors and
doing new things,
because we are curious,
and curiosity keeps leading us
down new paths".**
Walt Disney

Teachers open the door, you enter by yourself.

October

> Where there is no enemy within there are no enemies at all.
> *African proverb*

MONDAY 21 Trafalgar Day

Begin by taking small risks

TUESDAY 22

Life is too important to be taken seriously

WEDNESDAY 23

Prepare to succeed

THURSDAY 24

Develop an attitude of confidence

 The person who sows a beautiful thought
in the mind of another renders the world
a greater service than that rendered by
all the faultfinders combined.
Napoleon Hill

A man's life is what his thoughts make of it.
Marcus Aurelius

October

An open mind leaves a chance that a worthwhile thought will drop into it.

FRIDAY 25

Happy times are best when shared

SATURDAY 26

Challenge your own limits

SUNDAY 27

Summertime ends

I hated every minute of the training, but I said, "Don't quit.
Suffer now, and live the rest of your life as a champion."
Muhammad Ali

About Gossip

If you didn't see it with your own eyes,
and hear it with your own ears,
don't invent it with your small mind,
and share it with your big mouth.

October

MONDAY 28

Get into communication with people in your life

TUESDAY 29

Celebrate everything you can

WEDNESDAY 30

Curiosity will lead you down a new path

THURSDAY 31

Take time to build strong relationships

Our decision to walk creates the path ahead.

**Greatness is the result of
Caring more
than others think is wise,
Risking more
than others think is safe,
Dreaming more
than others think is practical,
and Expecting more
than others think is possible.**

Goals for November

The only thing that overcomes hard luck, is hard work.

November

Goals are dreams with deadlines.

FRIDAY 1

Your life is a message to the world

SATURDAY 2

Growing old beats the alternative!

SUNDAY 3

Your children get only one childhood

Life lived for tomorrow will always be just a day away from being realised.

November

MONDAY 4

All that truly matters in the end is that you loved

TUESDAY 5

Guy Fawkes Night

"Pennies for the Guy!"

Miracles await you everywhere

WEDNESDAY 6

Envy is a waste of time. You already have all you need

THURSDAY 7

The best is yet to come

FRIDAY 8

From serenity comes gentleness

In taking revenge, a man is but even with his enemy; but in passing it over, he is superior.

Sir Francis Bacon

November

Integrity rings like fine glass, true clear and reassuring.

Pam Brown

SATURDAY 9

Your thoughts determine how you feel

SUNDAY 10   Rememberence Sunday

Lest We Forget

They went with songs to the battle, they were young.
Straight of limb, true of eyes, steady and aglow.
They where staunch to the end, against odds uncounted,
They fell with their faces to the foe.
They shall grow not old, as we that are left grow old:
Age shall not weary them, nor the years condemn.
At the going down of the sun and in the morning,
We will remember them.

A grateful heart is one who lived through trials along the way
Who found the strength to look ahead and face a brand new day
A grateful heart is one who knows that sorrows do not last
A morning brings a ray of hope to chase away the past
A grateful heart will always be much stronger than the rest
For they have weathered every storm and conquered every test.

J. Lemming

Actions speak louder than words, ... but not nearly as often.

Mark Twain

Children learn what they live

If a child lives with criticism, he learns to condemn.
If a child lives with hostility, he learns to fight.
If a child lives with fear, he learns to be apprehensive.
If a child lives with pity, he learns to feel sorry for himself.
If a child lives with ridicule, he learns to be shy.
If a child lives with jealousy, he learns what envy is.
If a child lives with shame, he learns to feel guilty.
If a child lives with encouragement, he learns to be confident.
If a child lives with tolerance, he learns to be patient.
If a child lives with praise, he learns to be appreciative
If a child lives with acceptance, he learns to love.
If a child lives with approval, he learns to like himself.
If a child lives with recognition,
he learns that it is good to have a goal.
If a child lives with sharing,
he learns about generosity.
If a child lives with honesty and fairness,
he learns what truth and justice are.
If a child lives with security,
he learns to have faith in himself and in those about him.
If a child lives with friendliness,
he learns that the world is a nice place in which to live.
If you live with serenity,
your child will live with peace of mind.

We change the world by teaching our children.

Forgive the past.
Live the present.
Create the future.

The art of forgetting is a gift of great freedom.

November

Have a Nice Day

Every time you smile at someone, it is ∞
action of love, a gift to that person, a beautiful thing. *Mother Teresa*

MONDAY 11   Rememberence Day

Often, silence is the best answer

TUESDAY 12

Life always gives you a another chance

WEDNESDAY 13

Be on time

We must be silent before we can listen.
We must listen before we can learn.
We must learn before we can prepare.
We must prepare before we can serve.
We must serve before we can lead.
William Arthur Ward

Watch your manner of speech if you wish to develop a peaceful state of mind.
Start each day by affirming peaceful, contented and happy attitudes
and your days will tend to be pleasant and successful.
Norman Vincent Peale

November

A birth cert shows that you were born
A death cert shows that you died;
A photo album shows that you lived

THURSDAY 14

A balanced life is a gift we give ourselves

FRIDAY 15

Life would be dull without human error

SATURDAY 16

Assess your strengths accurately

SUNDAY 17

In each of us there is a little of all of us

Three things that never return: the past,
the missed opportunity, the spoken word.

Age does not protect you from love.
But love, to some extent, protects you from age.

Jeanne Moreau

November

If you think adventure is dangerous, try procrastination – its lethal.
Paul Coelho

MONDAY 18

Each day you are given an opportunity to be grateful

TUESDAY 19

Your life is filled with wonderful people

WEDNESDAY 20

Watch a 'feel good' movie

THURSDAY 21

You are supported by the love and abundance of the universe

**The secret of making something work in your lives
is, first of all, the deep desire to make it work.
Then the faith and belief that it can work.
Then to hold that clear definite vision in your consciousness
and see it working out step by step,
without one thought of doubt or disbelief.**
Eileen Caddy

Life loves to be taken by the lapel and told, 'I'm with you Kid. Lets go'.
Maya Angelou

THE POWER OF 1

One song can spark a moment,
One flower can wake the dream, One tree can
start a forest, One bird can herald spring.

One smile begins a friendship,
One handclasp lifts a soul, One star can guide
a ship at sea, One word can frame the goal.

One vote can change a nation,
One sunbeam lights a room, One candle wipes
out darkness, One laugh will conquer gloom.

One step must start each journey.
One word must start each prayer, One hope will
raise our spirits, One touch can show you care.

One voice can speak with wisdom,
One heart can know what's true, One life can
make a difference, You see, it's up to you!

Do not wait for leaders. Do it alone, person to person.
Mother Teresa

November

Even the smallest grain of rice will tip the scales.

FRIDAY 22

Understand yourself better in order to better understand others

SATURDAY 23

Be generous with your time

On Joy and Sorrow

Your joy is your sorrow unmasked. And the selfsame well from which your laughter rises was oftentimes filled with your tears. And how else can it be? The deeper that sorrow carves into your being, the more joy you can contain. Is not the cup that holds your wine the very cup that was burned in the potter's oven? And is not the lute that soothes your spirit, the very wood that was hollowed with knives? When you are joyous, look deep into your heart and you shall find it is only that which has given you sorrow that is giving you joy. When you are sorrowful look again in your heart, and you shall see that in truth you are weeping for that which has been your delight.

Some of you say, "Joy is greater than sorrow," and others say, "Nay, sorrow is the greater." But I say unto you, they are inseparable. Together they come, and when one sits, alone with you at your board, remember that the other is asleep upon your bed. Verily you are suspended like scales between your sorrow and your joy. Only when you are empty are you at standstill and balanced. When the treasure-keeper lifts you to weigh his gold and his silver, needs must your joy or your sorrow rise or fall.

Kahil Gibran

'Venture not to defend what your judgement doubts of'.

November

What a lovely surprise to discover how un-lonely being alone can be.

Ellen Burstyn

SUNDAY 24

We all have more potential than we could ever dream about

BE A WINNER

The Winner is always part of the answer.
The Loser is always part of the problem.

The Winner always has a program.
The Loser always has an excuse.

The Winner says "Let me do it for you."
The Loser says "That is not my Job".

The Winner sees an answer for every problem.
The Loser sees a problem in every answer.

The Winner sees a green near every sand trap.
The Loser sees two or three sand traps near every green.

The Winner says "It may be difficult. but it is possible."
The Loser says "It may be possible, but it's too difficult."

Champions aren't made in gyms.
Champions are made from something they have deep inside them,
a desire, a dream, a vision.
The have to have the skill, and the will.
But the will must be stronger than the skill.

Muhammad Ali

Take hold lightly; let go lightly.
This is one of the greatest secrets of felicity in love.

Spanish Proverb

November

**Worry looks around
Sorry looks back
Faith looks up
Hope looks forward.**

MONDAY 25

Think big thoughts, but relish small pleasures

TUESDAY 26

Strive for excellence, not perfection

WEDNESDAY 27

Leave everything a little better than you found it

THURSDAY 28

Focus on making things better, not bigger

Cleansing
Blessing

I bathe myself in generosity, appreciation, praise and gratitude for my fellow beings, self-acceptance, and enlightened understanding of all life experiences.

I cleanse myself of all selfishness, resentment, critical feelings for my fellow beings, self-condemnation, and misinterpretation of my life experiences.

November

Mistakes are the portals of discovery.
James Joyce

FRIDAY 29

Want it more than anything? Xcelerate your efforts

SATURDAY 30

Never cut what can be untied

Christmas Shopping List

1. The Irish Get Up And Go Diary 2014
2.
3.
4.
5.
6.
7.
8.
9.
10.

**If you are not willing to risk the usual,
you have to settle for the ordinary.**
Jim Rohn

Goals for December

Even if I don't reach all my goals, I've gone higher than I would have if I hadn't set any.

Danielle Fotopoulis

To remember how to be who you really are,
learn from the tree.
It does not spend its day running from task to task,
trying to get everything done and
trying to please everyone.
It does not care what I say about it, or what you think.
No matter what, it is and remains the tree.
It serves its purpose,
it lives long, and it stands proud and beautiful
being exactly what it is.

This we know:
all things are connected like the blood that unites us.
We did not weave the web of life,
we are merely a strand of it.
Whatever we do to the web, we do to ourselves

Chief Seattle

December

The price of greatness is responsibility
Winston Churchill

SUNDAY 1

Be at peace with your age, it is the right age for you

Success is speaking words of praise,
In cheering other people's ways.
In doing just the best you can,
With every task and every plan.
It's silence when your speech would hurt,
Politeness when your neighbours' curt.
It's deafness when the scandal flows,
And sympathy with others' woes.
It's loyalty when duty calls,
It's courage when disaster falls.
It's patience when the hours are long,
It's found in laughter and in song.
It's in the silent time of prayer,
In happiness and in despair.
In all of life and nothing less,
We find the thing we call success.

Let go of the past and go for the future. Go confidently in the direction of your dreams. Live the life you imagined.

Henry David Thoreau

December

There are two lasting
bequests we can give
our children: one is
roots, the other is wings.
Hodding Carter

MONDAY 2

Never give up on anybody. Miracles happen every day

TUESDAY 3

Enjoy life, wherever you are and whatever you're doing

WEDNESDAY 4

Stand firm for what is right

THURSDAY 5

It is better to try than to hope

 **Middle age is when you're sitting at home
on a Saturday night and the telephone rings
and you hope it isn't for you.**
Ogden Nash

The truth that makes men free is, for the most part,
the truth which men prefer not to hear.
Herbert Agar

December

FRIDAY 6

Put yourself at the top of your commitment list

SATURDAY 7

To visualize the end result has great power; practice it

SUNDAY 8

Allow yourself to dream

Spread love where ever you go
First of all in your house.
Give love to your children, your wife or husband,
to a next door neighbour.
Let no one ever come to you without leaving better and happier.
Be the living expression of Gods kindness,
kindness in your face,
kindness in your eyes,
kindness in your smile,
kindness in a warm greeting.

Mother Teresa

True leaders don't create followers, they create more leaders.
J sakiya sandifer

December

Faith is to believe what you do not see; the reward for this faith is to see what you believe.
Saint Augustine

MONDAY 9

No matter how difficult it seems now, it will get easier

TUESDAY 10

If you cannot speak good about somebody, rather say nothing

WEDNESDAY 11

The universe offers abundance in everything

THURSDAY 12

Encourage a child to be creative

FRIDAY 13

Time to put up the Christmas tree

The person who pulls the oars has no time to rock the boat.

December

Expect the best
plan for the wors
and prepare to b
surprised.

SATURDAY 14

Delegate tasks to capable others

SUNDAY 15

Love those who do not love you, for they may change

I'm gonna be a Bear

In this life I'm a woman,
In my next life I would like to come back as a bear.
When you're a bear, you get to hibernate.
You do nothing but sleep for six months.
I could deal with that.
Before you hibernate, you're supposed to eat yourself stupid.
I could deal with that too.
When you're a girl bear, you birth your children (who are the size of walnuts)
while you're sleeping, and wake to partially grown, cute, cuddly cubs.
I could definitely deal with that.
If you're a Momma bear, everyone knows you means business.
You swat anyone who bothers your cubs.
If your cubs get out of line, you swat them to.
I could deal with that.
If you're a bear, your mate expects you to wake up growling.
He expects you will have hairy legs and excess body fat.
Yup, i'm gonna be a bear.

December

He is happiest, be he king or peasant, who finds peace in his own home.

Wolfgang von Goethe

MONDAY 16

Spare a thought for someone less fortunate

TUESDAY 17

Send your loved one flowers. Think of a reason later

WEDNESDAY 18

It is hope that heals hopelessness

THURSDAY 19

There is no wisdom in cynicism

We must develop and maintain the capacity to forgive.
He who is devoid of the power to forgive, is devoid of the power to love.
There is some good in the worst of us and
some evil in the best of us.
When we discover this,
we are less prone to hate our enemies.

Martin Luther King

 # December

Holding a grudge is letting someone live rent free in your head.

FRIDAY 20

The best things in life are not things

SATURDAY 21

Take responsibility for the choices you make every day

SUNDAY 22

Treat your family as if they were special guests

Christmas waves it's magic wand over this world,
and behold, everything is softer
and more beautiful.

Norman Vincent Peale

The best of all gifts around any Christmas
tree is the presence of a happy family all
wrapped up in each other.

Burton Hills

 What if Christmas, he thought, doesn't come from a store.
What if Christmas, perhaps, means a little bit more. *Dr. Seuss*

C H R I S T M A S

I salute you.
I am your friend and my love for you goes deep.
There is nothing I can give you which you do not already have;
but there is much, very much which you can take.
Heaven cannot be experienced unless our hearts find love.
Take heaven.

No peace lies in the future which is not hidden in this instant.
Take peace.

The gloom of the world is but a shadow.
Behind it yet within our reach, is joy.
There is radiance and glory even in darkness,
could we but see, and to see, we only have to look.
I beseech you to look...

Life is so generous a giver, but we, judging its gifts by their coverings,
cast them away as heavy or hard.
Remove the covering and you will find beneath
it a living splendour woven of love,
wisdom and power.

Welcome it, grasp it and you touch the angel's hand that brings it to you.
Everything we call a trial, a sorrow or a duty, the angel's hand is there;
the gift is there as well as the wonder of an overshadowing presence.

Our joys too – be not content with them as joys,
as they too, conceal divine gifts.
Life is so full of meaning and purpose,
so full of beauty beneath its covering which cloaks your heaven.

Courage then, claim it – that is all.
Courage you have, and the knowledge that we are
pilgrims together wending our way home.
And so at Christmas time I greet you.
Not quite as the world sends greetings,
but with profound esteem and with the prayer that for you now
the day breaks in its fullest glory...

Fra Giovanni
1513 A.D.

December

Christmas is a time for giving; remember those in need.

MONDAY 23

Seek to understand before being understood

TUESDAY 24

Its Christmas Eve; Enjoy a Silent Night

WEDNESDAY 25

Peace comes from within, do not seek it without

THURSDAY 26

Visit family and friends

A Hundred years from now it will not matter what my bank account was, the sort of house I lived in, or the kind of car I drove . . . but, the world may be different because I was important in the life of a child.

 # December

Happiness is when you think, what you say, and what you do, are in harmony.

Mahatma Gandhi

FRIDAY 27

Avoid mediocrity and complacency

SATURDAY 28

Don't postpone joy

SUNDAY 29

Generate confidence

Master Yourself

If you are all interested in mastery, and who is not interested,
then become interested in Self Mastery.
Don't waste your time in trying to dominate others.
The effort to dominate creates conflict.
The whole world is full of it.
Even when you love a woman or a man, the mind starts its cunning ways,
to dominate, to possess, to control the freedom of the other..... for fear
that if you don't, you yourself will be dominated and controlled.
Master yourself, master your fears, and you are free.

Learn of the skilfull; he that teaches himself has a fool for his master.
Benjamin Franklin

December

Create a
comfortable home
from which to
launch your adventures

MONDAY 30

Listen, Listen, Listen...

TUESDAY 31

Never deprive someone of hope; it might be all they have

To laugh often and to love much;
to win the respect of intelligent persons
and the affection of children;
to earn the appreciation of honest citizens
and endure the betrayal of false friends;
to appreciate beauty;
to find the best in others;
to give of oneself;
to leave the world a bit better, whether by a healthy child,
a garden patch or a redeemed social condition;
to have played and laughed with enthusiasm
and sing with exultation;
to know even one life has breathed easier because you have lived –
this is to have succeeded.

Ralph Waldo Emerson

Slow dance

Have you ever watched kids on a merry go round,
Or listened to the rain slapping on the ground?
Ever followed a butterfly's erratic flight
Or gazed at the sun in the fading light?
You better slow down, don't dance so fast,
Time is short, the music wont last....
Do you run through each day, saying "I really must fly"
when you ask "how are you?", do you hear the reply?
When your day is done do you lie in your bed
with the next days chores running through your head?
You better slow down don't dance so fast,
Time is short, the music wont last .....
Ever told your child we'll do it tomorrow
and in your haste not see his sorrow?
Ever lost touch, see a good friendship die
'cos you never had time to call and say 'hi'...
You better slow down don't dance so fast,
Time is short, the music wont last.....
When you run so fast to get somewhere
you miss the fun of getting there.
When you worry and hurry through your day
its an unopened gift, thrown away.

Life is not a race, so take it slower
hear the music before the song is over.

What we call the beginning is often the end.
And to make an end is to make a beginning.
The end is where we start from.
T. S. Eliot

UNTIL WE MEET AGAIN

Order for Great Britain's Get Up And Go Diary 2014
(PLEASE PRINT IN BLOCK LETTERS)

Please send me _____ copy/copies of 2014 Diary

£8 each + £2 P&P per copy. A purchase of 10 or more diaries: P&P £1 per copy

NAME _____

ADDRESS _____

_____

_____

I enclose Cheque/Postal Order to the value of _____

Signature _____

Contact No./Email _____

Forward your order to: Get Up And Go Publications Ltd.
8 Burma Road, Strandhill, Co. Sligo, Ireland. (Brendan Sands +353861788631)
Everyone would love to get a Get Up And Go Diary for Christmas
Order online at www.getupandgodiary.com

Order for Great Britain's Get Up And Go Diary 2014
(PLEASE PRINT IN BLOCK LETTERS)

Please send me _____ copy/copies of 2014 Diary

£8 each + £2 P&P per copy. A purchase of 10 or more diaries: P&P £1 per copy

NAME _____

ADDRESS _____

_____

_____

I enclose Cheque/Postal Order to the value of _____

Signature _____

Contact No./Email _____

Forward your order to: Get Up And Go Publications Ltd.
8 Burma Road, Strandhill, Co. Sligo, Ireland. (Brendan Sands +353861788631)
Everyone would love to get a Get Up And Go Diary for Christmas
Order online at www.getupandgodiary.com